# The Northeast Region

**by Victoria Leonardo**

## Table of Contents

# Introduction

The United States has fifty states. The states can be grouped into **regions**. Each region has several states. Each region is part of the United States.

CANADA

MAINE

VERMONT

NEW HAMPSHIRE

Adirondack Mountains

Lake Ontario

MASSACHUSETTS

NEW YORK

RHODE ISLAND

CONNECTICUT

Appalachian Mountains

Lake Erie

PENNSYLVANIA

NEW JERSEY

Washington, D. C.

DELAWARE

WEST VIRGINIA

MARYLAND

VIRGINIA

▲ **The Northeast region is a region of the United States.**

The **Northeast** region is one of the regions.

*Atlantic Ocean*

cities

environment

government

history

native people

Northeast

regions

seacoast

suburbs

See the Glossary on page 30.

3

# What Is the Northeast Region?

The Northeast region is part of the United States. The Northeast region has eleven states. Washington, D.C. is in the Northeast region. Washington, D.C. is not a state.

▲ Washington D.C. is in the Northeast.

New York is the largest state in the Northeast. Rhode Island is the smallest state in the Northeast.

**Did You Know?**

Delaware was the first state.

▲ Lake Placid is in New York.

▲ Newport is a city in Rhode Island.

Washington, D.C. is in the Northeast region. Washington, D.C. is not a state. Washington, D.C. is a city.

Washington, D.C. is the capital of the United States. The national **government** is in Washington, D.C. The national government is the government of the United States.

**It's a Fact**
D.C. means
District of Columbia.

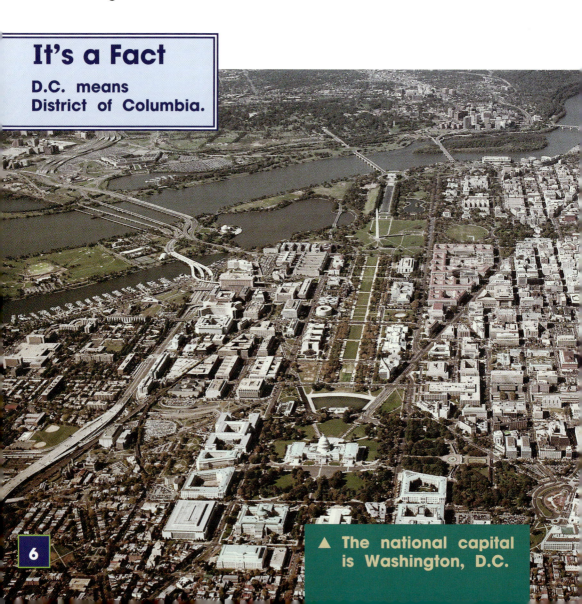

▲ The national capital is Washington, D.C.

Washington, D.C. is named for George Washington. The Washington Monument is in Washington, D.C.

## People to Know

**George Washington was the first president of the United States.**

The Washington ▲ Monument is in the national capital.

# What Is the Environment of the Northeast Region?

The Northeast region has mountains. Mountains are part of the **environment**.

The Appalachian Mountains are in the Northeast. The Appalachians are old mountains. They are about 680 million years old.

## Did You Know?

The Appalachian Mountains are about 1,000 miles (2,400 kilometers) long. Some of the Appalachian Mountains are in the Northeast. Some of the Appalachians are not in the Northeast.

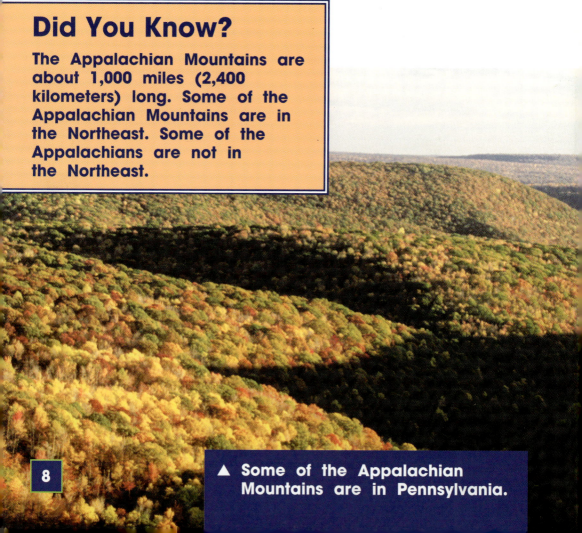

▲ Some of the Appalachian Mountains are in Pennsylvania.

The Adirondack Mountains are in the Northeast. The Adirondack Mountains are in New York.

The Northeast region is along the Atlantic Ocean. The ocean is part of the environment.

The Northeast region has a **seacoast**. Most of the seacoast is sandy. The seacoast is part of the environment.

▲ **The seacoast of New Jersey is sandy.**

▲ **The seacoast of Maine is very rocky.**

The seacoast has many bays. Bays are parts of the ocean. Bays have land around much of their water.

▲ **The Chesapeake Bay is in the Northeast.**

The seacoast has peninsulas. Peninsulas are pieces of land. Peninsulas have water on three sides.

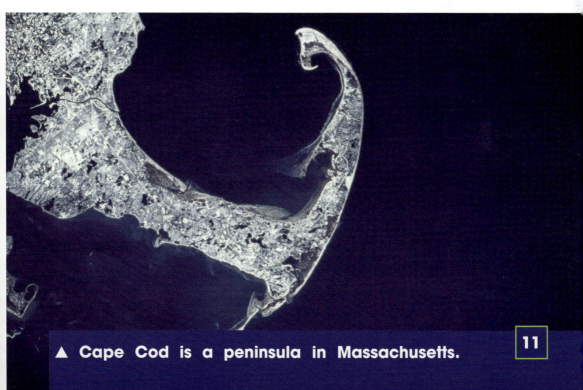

▲ **Cape Cod is a peninsula in Massachusetts.**

11

The Northeast region has lakes. Lakes are part of the environment.

Lake Ontario is in the Northeast region. Lake Ontario is one of the Great Lakes. Part of Lake Erie is in the Northeast region. Lake Erie is one of the Great Lakes.

Lake Champlain is very large. Lake Champlain is not a Great Lake. Lake Champlain is in Vermont, New York, and Canada.

## Did You Know?

The Niagara River is between Lake Ontario and Lake Erie. Niagara Falls is on the Niagara River.

▲ Lake Champlain has about eighty islands.

The Northeast region has rivers. Rivers are part of the environment. The chart shows six important rivers in the Northeast.

| River | Where | How Long |
|---|---|---|
| 1. Connecticut River | Connecticut, Massachusetts, New Hampshire, Vermont | About 405 miles (652 kilometers) |
| 2. Delaware River | Delaware, New Jersey, New York, Pennsylvania | About 410 miles (660 kilometers) |
| 3. Hudson River | New York and New Jersey | About 315 miles (506 kilometers) |
| 4. Potomac River | Maryland, Virginia, Washington, D.C., West Virginia | About 413 miles (665 kilometers) |
| 5. Saint Lawrence River | New York and Canada | About 1,900 miles (3,058 kilometers) |
| 6. Susquehanna River | Maryland, New York, Pennsylvania | About 444 miles (715 kilometers) |

## Did You Know?

The Erie Canal opened in 1825. The canal went between the Hudson River and Lake Erie.

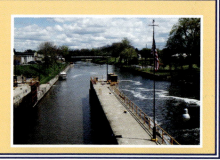

The Northeast region has seasons. Seasons are part of the environment.

▲ Summer in the Northeast can be hot.

▲ Fall in the Northeast can be cool.

▲ Winter in the Northeast can be very cold.

▲ Spring in the Northeast can be warm.

# What Is the History of the Northeast Region?

**Native people** lived in the Northeast at first. Groups of native people lived in the Northeast. One group was the Iroquois. The Iroquois lived in what is now New York.

| History of the Northeast Region | | | |
|---|---|---|---|
| **Before 1620** | **1620** | **1775–1783** | **1840–1930** |
| Only native people lived in the Northeast. | First colonists came to the Northeast. | Colonists and England fought the American Revolution. Many battles were in the Northeast. | Immigrants came to the Northeast. |

## It's a Fact

The Iroquois and seven other groups made one government. The government was the Iroquois Confederacy.

The Iroquois lived in longhouses. Longhouses were built with tree trunks. Longhouses were built with bark from the trees. Many families lived in one longhouse.

▲ Iroquois longhouses were made from trees.

Colonists came to the Northeast region. The colonists came from England. The first colonists were Pilgrims. The Pilgrims came to what is now Massachusetts. They built the colony of Plymouth.

## Learn More

Learn more about the Pilgrims at Plymouth. Visit **www.plimoth.org**

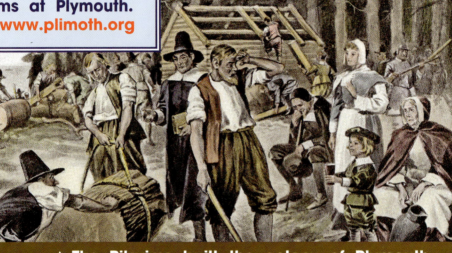

▲ **The Pilgrims built the colony of Plymouth.**

## It's a Fact

The Pilgrims came in 1620. They came on a ship named the *Mayflower*.

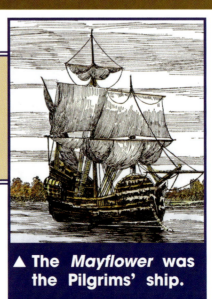

▲ The *Mayflower* was the Pilgrims' ship.

Many other colonists came to the Northeast. Some of the colonists wanted their own church. Other colonists wanted a better life.

▲ **Quakers came to what is now Pennsylvania.**

England ruled the colonies. England asked the colonists to pay taxes. England needed the money from taxes.

Many colonists did not want to pay taxes. Many colonists did not want England to rule.

▲ Colonists wanted to be free from England.

The colonists fought a war with England. The war was the American Revolution. The colonists won the war.

## It's a Fact

**The colonists wanted a new country. The country was the United States of America.**

▲ The colonists fought the American Revolution.

Many immigrants came to the Northeast. Immigrants are people who come from other countries.

Many immigrants were poor people. These people wanted to find work. Many of the immigrants did not speak English.

**Did You Know?**
Many immigrants came on ships. The ships came into New York Harbor.

▲ Immigrants came to Ellis Island.

The immigrants worked at many jobs. They worked many hours every day. Children worked many hours every day.

▲ **Immigrant children worked many hours.**

The immigrants built railroads and schools. The immigrants worked in mines. The immigrants were farmers.

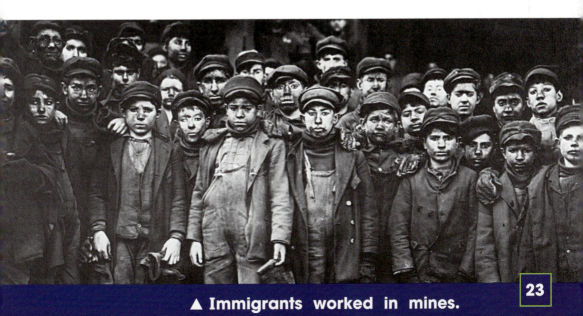

▲ **Immigrants worked in mines.**

# What Is the Northeast Region Like Today?

Some people live in small towns. More people live in large **cities**. The towns around the cities are **suburbs**.

The chart shows five cities in the Northeast. They are the largest cities in the Northeast. More people live in suburbs around these cities.

| City | State | Population |
| --- | --- | --- |
| Baltimore | Maryland | 651,154 |
| Boston | Massachusetts | 589,141 |
| New York | New York | 8,008,278 |
| Philadelphia | Pennsylvania | 1,517,550 |
| Washington, | D.C. | 572,059 |

## Solve This

Which city is the largest city? Which city is the smallest city? Which cities have populations of less than one million?

answers: New York; Washington, D.C.; Baltimore, Boston, Washington D.C.

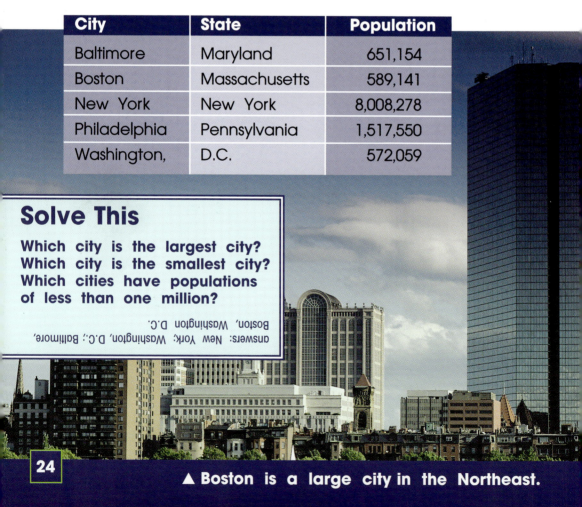

▲ Boston is a large city in the Northeast.

New York is the largest city in the Northeast. There are many other large cities in the Northeast. People live and work in these cities.

## Then and Now

**About 22,000 people lived in New York in 1750. How many people live in New York now?**

▲ New York is a large city in the Northeast.

People do many kinds of work in the Northeast. Many people do manufacturing work. Manufacturing means making things. People make steel, machines, and medicine.

▲ **People make plane engines.**

People work in banks in the Northeast. People work in hospitals in the Northeast.

▲ **This hospital is in Massachusetts.**

Computers are important in the Northeast. Many people work with computers.

▲ **People work with computers in the Northeast.**

The Northeast has many universities. Universities are schools. People go to universities after high school.

▲ **Yale University is in Connecticut.**

27

The Northeast region is part of the United States. The Northeast has land and water. The Northeast has seasons.

| area of the United States |
| --- |
| eleven states |
| Washington, D.C. |

**What Is the Northeast Region?**

**The Northeast Region**

| mountains |
| --- |
| Atlantic Ocean |
| seacoast |
| lakes |
| rivers |
| seasons |

**What Is the Environment of the Northeast Region?**

The **history** of the Northeast is very important. The Northeast has big cities. People do many different kinds of work.

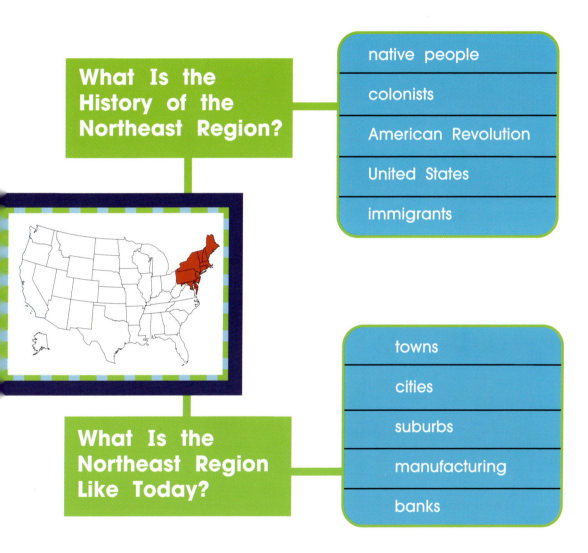

What Is the History of the Northeast Region?

- native people
- colonists
- American Revolution
- United States
- immigrants

What Is the Northeast Region Like Today?

- towns
- cities
- suburbs
- manufacturing
- banks

## Think About It

1. What is the Northeast region?
2. Tell about the environment of the Northeast.
3. Tell about the history of the Northeast.

29

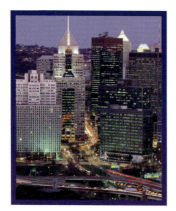

**cities** very large communities

*Pittsburgh and New York are cities in the Northeast.*

**environment** land, water, and seasons

*Mountains are part of the Northeast environment.*

**government** laws for people

*The United States government is in Washington, D.C.*

**history** what happened in the past

*Immigrants are part of the Northeast region's history.*

**native people** people who live in a place first

*The Iroquois were native people in the Northeast.*

**Northeast** a region in the United States

*The Northeast region has eleven states.*